The Road to Mellon Udrigle

*glints and skinkles in a land
of water and stone*

Angus D.H. Ogilvy

Published by Hermit Crab,
30/5 Polwarth Crescent Edinburgh EH11 1HN
hermitcrabpoems@gmail.com

ISBN # 978-0-9572764-2-0

Set in Cambria
Printed by printondemand-worldwide

Cover photography by Angus Ogilvy

Acknowledgements:

Poems in this collection previously published as follows:

Abe and *Man and Dog* in **Words 1***;*
Dan in **Words 2***;*
Bouquet in **Words 2** and **Into The Forest, An Anthology of Tree Poems** edited by Mandy Haggith (Saraband);
Larks in **Words 8***;*
Lament and *Grouse* in **Chapman 35/36***;*
Anent the Kirk's Intent Anent Anent and *The Road to Mellon Udrigle* in **Making Waves, stories and poems from The Federation of Writers (Scotland)**(New Voices Press);
Corrievreckan and *The Shock of the Mocked* in **Hebridean Diary of a Serial Sailor** *by* **Cully Pettigrew**

To

Neil

Contents

Foreword

The poems in this collection share a common provenance: the land and culture of my native Scotland. Though I spent many years living and working in what many Scots referred to in my childhood as 'exotic climes' in Asia and Africa, Scotland always remained the source to which I had to return at regular intervals for sustenance and in which I am now again happily resident. The land, its climate and its culture has influenced me from childhood in such a way that I was, and remain, 'forever shifted'.

Special Thanks

I am indebted to:

Peter McDade for his eagle-eyed editing skills.

Carol Ogilvy for her help with the cover and ongoing advice.

The School of Poets where some of the poems had their initial 'airing'.

Previous collections by *Angus Ogilvy*
published by Hermit Crab:

Lights in the Constellation of the Crab

House Clearing by Moonlight

the proceeds from both of which go to
Maggie's Cancer Caring Centres

Angus Ogilvy can be contacted at:

hermitcrabpoems@gmail.com

Glints

Onywhaur in Gallawa'

He hadna thocht
he wis whaur he wis,
but he wis.

An' if he hadna bin whaur he wis,
but wis whaur he thocht he'd bin,
he'd no hae bin whaur they fun' him,

jist as he wis,
whaur he had nae mind tae be –

a' things backweys,
the wey they'd bin
afore he kent
he wis onywhaur at a'.

Stopping in Assynt

So,
the day hangs;
midges swarm by slow water;
a bee hums at a red clover
somewhere over to my left.

Slapping at old rock,
the Atlantic, on its back,
is napping over deep time.

Residual fear of this easy stillness
niggles me to move about,
trample the ground on heather and sphagnum,
green mounds of lazy beds,
search for something,
stir things up.

With a struggle I suppress it,
recline beneath the cumulus sky
tingling with invisible birds.

Already I am in the right place:
the lochan disturbed by one trout's ripple,
a spider walking high-wire in a zone of its own,
nonchalant sheep rasping at grasses
on the side of this dependable hill.

Like a warm stone,
I lie silent without the language of wind.

Outlier

He was bred amongst the margin dwellers
on the edge-lands, salt washed, shaped by wind,
ancient accretions of crystallised kin,
and an ocean's tug to strangeness and dispersal.

He wears the symbols that he did not form,
traces them, weathered, in the reused stones
he borrows from a crumbling wall, the songs
his forebears sang into the storms.

In the landscape of rust all things are aged:
infants exude the aura of old souls,
and saplings stoop with what prevails –
a weight of struggles long since reaped and turned
on a land upwelling from saturation,
nursing a thirst that will not be assuaged.

Man and Dog

Shaw passed out slowly
from the twilight of his eyes
into a darkness quite devoid of shadow.
His dog, which shared his shrinking years,
now also shared the same affliction.
Blind man; blind dog.

Often we passed them miles from home
in distant corners of the parish
where the views were finest,
feeling out the road, defying nothing;

for each unaware that both
now shared the darkness of the day,
relied upon the other's eyes
to guide them safely on their way.

Out Back

A movement amongst trees
snapped stick
bloodbeat.

Attention usurps
with the luck luck luck
of a grass grown stream

the backwash of a breeze
through leaves
prattling rain that stops
with silence.

There's no complete return
from wilderness
its webs unearth neglected sense
what's conscious is forever shifted.

You won't unsnap
that stick you broke
dissolve a movement
into figment.

Sure as faith
it is presence
shapes the path I go
the heart's placebo.

This Land; A Reawakening

I smell this land.
Even when I am not in it

I am held by the aroma of its moon
suspended in a nook of trees, a cleft of hills;

its wood smoke in the morning breeze
was juniper, and should be still.

I know the full, familiar scent
its scuffling creatures make through leaves;

the sweetness in the sweat of burdens
carried on its web of ways, the ways I went

conveyed by wafts of starlight in its gloaming days
on mossed paths worn to passages down roots of trees.

I know the redolence of green
exuding from its wet, wet earth,

that sifts from streams its clearest breath
to startle memory.

I atomize the essence of this land
into the perfume of its sky against my hand,

a myrtle trace to stir affinity
I have no need to truly understand.

Winter Solstice On Springbank Hill

One gable end, and two arthritic trees
bent landward to the sloping of the field;
this plot uncultivated for the sidhe,
whose wind-songs shrill in clefts of opened stone.

The sharp hill-grass is rasped by black-backed stirks
with steaming snouts and pool-dark eyes transfixed
on mounds of feed for growing beef. Crows crave
the place from flocks of startled lapwings, squabbling geese.

But for the low sun, I'd have missed the three
roe deer come leaping from the gully
by the spring, and ripple through that herd
of stolid beasts like emissaries of
the other place beyond the veil of freezing fog
condensing on the warm breath off the sea.

A Piece of Parachute

A dull hill in a winter gauze of mist,
a dark turf scar, the niff of paraffin,
and then a mess of mangled metal bits.

I stopped for breath, for no,
I hadn't climbed for this,
but poked around it crow-like nonetheless:

a plane smacked by a billion years of rock –
low-level exercise, lost from radar the month before
to whisps of wool, and scree, and windblown moss.

I'd heard about the pilots' deaths, the ball of fire;
blew silver smoke against my fingers to unsnap the cold.

I found a torn-off stretch of silken parachute
that might have meant ejection and escape,
the brake to make an impact stop, that failed.

I folded it and placed it in a pocket of my sack
to fill some future undetermined use
that was not waste, yet would be so,

then turned my back
and thumped my numb feet on towards the top.

On Dec 19 1979 an American F1-11E crashed on Craignaw in Galloway killing both pilots.

The Truant on Craigoch Tor

The long OM of the foghorn, whale song
ruminating in the belly of the sea;
from the bone's hollow comb, reverberation
root to limb, stirring my dream in the chestnut tree.

The old bull is bellowing round the bowl of its skull
into the milk that smothers the morning
like a clamped hand compressing to a dumb, dull
growl the roar in its gullet of some forlorn warning.

A droning engine stutters, looms, recedes,
returns to oscillate where earth and sky are one.

That pilot may be lost and found like me,
unmindful of his doom's proximity,
adrift, alone, through intermittent sound,
following convoluted calls where they should lead.

Abe

Abe the ploughman
lived on tractor and furrow;
a heart of the earth
with a face worn in claysmiles,
crusted hard and brown as soil.

Saw horse and engine,
oil and atoms;
lay fallow in his head,
unchanged as the land
through centuries of scoring.

Time ploughed his brow
and reaped the harvest of his head,
pure white beneath his cap.

He had no woman
till the spinster earth
took the essence of his body into her own;
a gentle seed to her gaping fertility.

As I watched him
through my boyhood window on spring mornings,
when the sun slowed his movements on the hill
into the snailing stillness of a painted landscape,
I saw a marriage, with a train of white feathers,
lost to perpetual endurance.

Lament

We masquerade a greatness
but we breed mourners
to a loud disconsolate music.
Our wild posturing is granite
from the dark sod moor
steeped into centuries of self neglect.
Our minds are layers of shifting patience;
our bones are filed by wind.

Our grudge held like a stump long dead,
preserved in simmering peat,
brags of a failure to succeed.
Old prides survive as drunkards, lords,
or weathered stones.

Our history is a brawl
that hacks its heroes from hard lies,
makes monumental glories of defeat,
a passion hot with prejudice
and legends of lost men.

From rage of purpose came a condign god
to grapple pleasure with the claw of guilt,
a carrion bird that looms his spectre through sag mists,
a brooding shadow on unconscienced joy.

Beside the warmth of winter fires
we laugh behind our camouflage of selves.
Our ringing songs are echoes from sad hills,
philosophy that slices to the pith,

succinct, hereditary, smiling in its face.

Our children curl in sleep.
Outside, the welcomed stranger watches ripples
on our dark still waters deep.

Eagle Rising

It launched from the slope on wings like rugs,
stalled us in the middle of a word.

It commandeered wind,
occupied sky,
made stones of rocks,
gave no quarter to shadow
on the stark earth.

Birch trees stilled
and looked to their roots;
the iron hill contracted
in its camouflage of rust.

At the centre of the world's eye,
we bowed beneath
those outstretched primaries,
fixed by fate, disinherited,
dumb.

The Rendezvous

I'll meet you,
when the time comes,
unprepared.

You'll fill me with
the shock of coincidence,

the just-so thusness
of how it is,

and I'll remember for an instant
in the rush that takes us

that all my life
I had longed for this
one so complete intensity.

Scots Quartz

black hill
grey sky
white stone

Bouquet

You brought me heather
that you'd gathered from the crest
of some eternal hill.

But being rootless, it decayed
in quiet stages
on the windowsill.

It brought me pain
to know you would have made
a gift
to me
of that whole purple mountain.

Meeting the Deer on Glas Mheall Mor

We stare
through transient
awareness, no thought as
tangible as silence, shadow,
windshift.

On the Island

Held with me
between the shock and the wonder,
an oyster-catcher strutting
with his hands behind his back
voicing his concerns,
blowing his vexations
through a child's first piccolo,
charging with his carrot of alarm.

I watch him conjure nightmares
in the evolutions of his three stone eggs
to shrivel seaweeds on the shingle bank
that he might dupe a passing crow.

Endless activity and frustration:
always the invention of another thing
to do, another fear, a found distraction,
lest a lurking nothingness confront existence,
reveal itself as certain as a cliff.

Better to be
with the dullness of ignorance
sheltered in conformities of stone.

Better to be
scurrying the greywackes, an anti-hero
screaming decoy presence as a charm.

Caught between
the shock and the wonder,

between the sea and its arc of emptiness,
wind decides the attitude of water,
wipes its moods across a passive sky,
brushes with the linger of a whisper
something that I ache to hear,
but cannot hold, and ponder why.

Terns at Horgabost

A moon-arc veering a streak's velocity
its tail acute as god's dividers
scalpels water's surface meniscus
with a red razor's delicacy
slicing for needle fish.

In the vector of the sky's blue edge
a five point star of Antarctic crystal
shrieking a *kee-yaah* sharp as a meteor spark
sickles through space at the apex of a ripple
resonating like a tuning fork.

I glide as pivot on the plane of my axis
head hood of darkness with an angel's wings

a parabola of paradise quivering to splinter
the symmetry of morning.

Grouse

Fierce from the heather flare of wings
all hollow vowelled on the pulsive air,
the call made rapid
rattling down the laugh's long throat.

Low level grouse
blur over contours at the edge of light,
make sheep to flex their knuckle heads,
are loud as engines on the honeyed moor.

One... two...
the thrash released in duplicate
from coils of root
turns catapult of bird to double thunder
and the thud of death.
In camouflage an eyeball smokes
behind the barrels of a butt.

Grouse are the victims of their own unnerve;
are decoys of themselves to false alarm;
are seldom seen
until, like men condemned,
they beat the air
and charge the skies unarmed.

Great Skua at the Point of Stoer

stone veined surf-skimmer
blood agate earth bird
moor-skulker
splinter off
a tide rush
ashore

scythe winged sea skudder parasitic pirate
swag swiper skooshing on a storm sail askew

spike-eyed rock scourer pilferer predator scourge of the colonies
scalp skelper mobster carrion scatter scrounger camouflaged
kamikaze kleptocrat of cliff stacks

obscure surge swooper
scream scooper
skite stooper

scavenger of
scat spewers

meat skewer

wind slicer

surf rider

skyspur
s
t
u
k
a

Laid to Restlessness

She said she'd be released to write a river
flowing from her own sad grasses, sand and stone
through sprinkled sunlight, painted darkness, driven rain;

and over lips of sultry pools beneath a sweep of trees,
chuckling every now and then, while pirouetting on a pebble
with a boatman balanced on a paper leaf, a feather
in a shallow reach where fish flip in a swish of silver.

She wished to muster all the waters from the troubled hill,
the bloodied moor, the oily bog, the blackened peat;
those stinging drops that splatter onto new turned fields
and seep down runnels under residues of tired snow;
the moist of mosses over spongy soil and wood.

She'd be carried by the current of its captured will,
escape the weight of stillness stuck in one last place without
the palliation of some slow dissolving drip-to-trickle,
running, rolling, rushing, gushing, bursting in a torrent –
free to be that always swirling, surging, singing sea
she knew that she was always meant to be.

Evening At Altanabradhan

We followed the path to the derelict mill,
where a wild burn spun on gneiss,
its incline borrowed for a grinding time
when clack stones turned on barley bere
or black oatmeal, and flour stoor coated
the milner's sark through fustiness of wetted wool,
seaweeds sweating the beach below.

We wondered how they'd borne their crops
from meagre rigs on horse or human back,
each stooping step against the slope
on bracken, boulders, turf and moss;
and why our fascination for abandoned forms
of need and will amongst the skail of glacial dross.

We recognised a common cause:
a bleached bone lying there,
both right and wrong, by broken walls,
and two couped wheels of sculpted stone,
all glistering silver from the turning sky,
held golden droppings of its falling sun.

Sheltering in East Kip Wood

I enter, on my hands and knees,
the half-light underneath the trees
through grey and rust,
crawl amongst wool tufts snagged on bark,
suspended filaments of seed and dust,
and, onto a bed of needles, stand at last.

There's scent of sanctuary in drying scat
and weeping pine, the pellet wraps
of hair and bone like entombed embryos;
a sense of aftermath around the rodent skull,
antler, melted candle, broken glass,
a bloom of feathers on the scuffed-out track.

The air-crack as I break a root
insinuates the forest is the wood
that rests within the stillness of the space,
while at its fringes storm winds rage.

Tuning Isobars

We didn't have a chimney
when we lived in the tropics,
so there never was any wind in it.

No wind in no chimney
gave the impression there was no air,
which was oppressive and smothered our sleep.

So we'd turn on the ceiling fan
to get the impression of wind in a chimney,
but something was wrong.

It wasn't at random, its rhythm a regular
pulse in the darkness, an artificial respirator,
in no sense alive.

It gave no impression of the beast outside
with its breath in the stonework –
then and again and again and then,

and the house as its instrument
skirling in tones through the drone in the wall:
music of home in the temperate zone.

On Berneray

This is how it is.

Walls dilapidate, doors disintegrate,
roofs rust through to their beams,
chimneys sever from smoke,
creel boats die slowly out of their element
down to the bone.

Yesterday's implements, no longer implemented,
nestle in nettle beds.

Each shell reshapes to be
precursor to the next.

Sky passes over, mostly blue, on nervy wind.
A cloud buffs a hill till it gleams.

Out there on the headlands
vestiges of chosen truths
abide as stones up-ended at determined angles
in offerings to reason and to speculation.

Here the no night air
spills courting songs of procreation,
the low light weepings of birds.

Up from a grey ditch the yellow iris springs.

Over unhurried gradients
the machair rolls on through the burial mounds

to a marigold, buttercup, bob cotton shore
for the lover, the plover, the meadow pipit, me.

No other voice responds from the dunes.

The only soul is the sea.

Risings

From Kirkaig's deep pools
fish flip to snatch flies, fall back
into clear darkness.

Cramond Island

Something primordial exults in me
to be beyond the causeway,
having walked on what was water
where the salt slip crackles with the last tide's dregs;

a hybrid place at peace with paradox,
not island nor peninsula
but both, part time, and twice a day
that severs its umbilical
according to the impulse of the moon.

Only the unsalvageable now remains,
fortified by weathered rock
and the sea's inconstant moat.

Sea birds screech vestigial spites,
an evolution of Jurassic feuds
played out on mudflats bubbling
and brimming with what is buried.

Carrion crows shell a derelict bunker
with guided molluscs, to gorge on mucus
once their guard is down.

We relish the solitude,
wade through wreaths of coppered bracken
over moss on dykes and ditches,
like ancient races hearing incantations
on the full winds off the Forth.

Be chary, ye that meddle here!
Tak tent the perfidie o' time!
Beware the surge tae interfere,
Lest ye be cast aff in yer prime!

Setting

This sky
is slate,

and I,
leaving,
looking
for mica,

a sparkle
of quartz,

or oils
of opal,

the hint
of a glint

of fool's gold.

Corrievreckan

Be careful should you lift the lid,
for here are torments
raging from the bones of ancients
boiling up through surface sclera
bulging with the lens of an obsidian eye
that turns in torques of tidal eddies;

breaching flukes of consternation
chucked up on their edge as standing waves
around subducting plates of flood and ebb;
mindstroms from dark undercurrents
roused to break in brimming scald-rings
blistering on a weeping skin of sea.

So I pass the Corrievreckan at slack water time,
and sail by on the safer side
through gentle swells in favourable wind,
as if no passions ever stirred
beneath such calm serenity.

Could I brave my heart to anchor there
on a rope of woven maiden's hair,
not knowing if my trust be pure
under that perigean moon?

In legend, Bhreacan, to prove his love, had to anchor for three days and nights in the location of the great tidal whirlpool. On the advice of wise men, he used three ropes: one of wool, one of hemp and one of maiden's hair. Each broke in turn and Bhreacan drowned. His body washed ashore and was buried in Uamh Bhreacan (the cave of Brecan) on Jura.

Cloudberries

Not long after the last cloud lifted from the mountain,
though skiffing it still with lingering wisps,
I came upon the averin growing bold
amongst the cold, damp mosses of the bealach
with heads held up in bursts of sunlight,
small knots of redness, hard on hairstalks,
mellowing to a misty orange, yellowing to highland gold;
and I noticed how they'd spread by stealth
through rhizomes running deep beneath the heather
like guarded truths secreted under covered beds.

I picked one off and smudged a musty juice
between my fingers, but I did not dare to taste,
suspicious of its tart and swagger set beside
the dull, the cowed, the camouflaged, the status quo,
and fearful of imagined poisons offered simply
in a feast of freedom, too wild, too pure,
too natural to be true.

Remembrance Day

The trees have rusted,
become arterial with rigored bone.
The leaves fall down.
The sky's washed pink as an abattoir floor.

Across the Meadows comes the thrum
of marching music.
The callants step out smartly, spit and shine,
down Forrest Road towards St. Giles,
a doubtful pedigree of tartan glories,
their banners bright with new dyes.

Dignitaries are assembling in poppy red;
the council, black;
the veterans with their ribbons,
somehow out of place on tweed,
their medals gold as autumn.

Two minutes are given to an inner distance,
numb as a bell that tolls in Leith.
The children stamp their feet.
A young recruit slumps to the street,
a parody of all the dead we try to summon,
and they leave him there.

I visualise an uncle's face
that sank through icy Arctic seas
with braid and buttons
on a bedroom wall.
The flags make limp apology

as all those battered dead
come filing up through generations,
ineffable numbers from textbook histories,
too huge for guilt.

And nor is this an exculpation.
How much flesh makes how much dust?
Here is an elegy of passing flowers
and bugle calls for carnal death
while all those clotted leaves fall down.

Over Ypres and Arnhem,
Bannockburn and Crecy,
Hiroshima and nineteen-eighty
the leaves fall down inexorably
as they always will.

Geese fly a liquid arrow overhead.
The loudest thing
is the silence.

On Cold Days

On cold, cold days old men grow tears.
Their eyes can't hold back anymore
the recognition of what's been done,
and what is not yet to do.

In a Cauld Pairt

It'll end in tears.
It ayeweys dis.

Ye've no sooner snecked it
than it's aff tae god kens whaur.

That's jist the wey it is.

An' whit are ye left wi'?
Jist whit ye had afore.

But worse.
Ye've had a taste o' whit ye fancy
an' noo it isnae there.

An' it feels like something's
tummled oot yer basket,
wi' you daein' nocht but thinkin'
ye had somethin' that ye hadnae,
an' the weight o' it still hings.

An' wha'da thoat it?

Oniewey,
ye'll be glad ye dinnae huv tae
fash yersel' aboot it oniemair,
an' jist get oan wi' whit ye huv.

Aye,
an thank yer lucky stars ye've goat it!

the gift of snow

is edge
subdued
to lip

the strident
kissed
to acquiesce
in silk

salutations
of strangers
shuffling
selfsame ways

one night of silver

flake
by trillion
flake

silence percolates

and stones
made soft

as if embraced
by slow, slow
scintillations
of accumulated
moss

On a Cross Country Line

Passing beneath small bridges there's that rush
of forced out-breath above the tracks
to interrupt the rattling respiration of the train.

Not being the usual air-streamed tube through tinted glass,
it's slow, and clear enough to note the hand cut tessellations
curving up precisely to the keystone of each arch,
as intricate as the drying ferns with root-holds
clinging in its white lime mortar cracks.

Under some there's constant trickling over mosses
brown as treacle where the sun won't touch,
holding droplets, hanging, shivering,
as the train wafts past.

These bridges are the routes to other life,
the links that lead to different rights of way
I share with lumbering cows and skittish sheep,
the post van bringing moods to shape the day.

Here's the inroad that could let me be of use,
the artery to explore another's need
that I would sever blindly with a speed screamed push
as some meeting over money supersedes.

December Boat Train

Crippled pigeons on stub feet
harry for handouts in Central Station.
The train grinds and shoogles through
the back ends of derelict sheds sprayed
with the cartoon calligraphy of yesterday's threats.

Everything is wet.

Gravel heaps trickle in pooled yards;
the gasometer, that long ago exhaled its last,
glistens with stains of seeped corruption.

We leave the city, wheezing through
another bronchial winter,
and enter a mudscape of steaming cattle
wallowing in cloying fields,
wheel-track hollows filled with dimpled rain,
trees lined up like oiled corals,
their barks the colour of soaked roads;
hills left caked in the grime of old snows.

Later, high on a sodden moor,
a drenched buzzard stands rooted in a dead sheep.

Out of the grey sky we descend towards a grey sea,
where a dank ferry waits to spread a white wave
pointing to another land.

No Measured Step

That old sage Lao Tse,
bending in the wind
with his action in no action,
knowing in unknowing,
was the one to say it first:

A journey of ten thousand miles
begins with a single step.

Now you see it everywhere;
at seminars for whatsit floggers
whose journeys are inclined to find
the Tao more usefully assigned
to yielding on the bottom line.

My journey starts
with no known step;
my action is no action.

More the advent of an urge,
a spring that wells,
a fluke of fears to trip me
on the impulse of the air.

There is no plodding footfall here,
no walking out upon a chosen route
that's plotted for adventures on the way.

I glide, alone, above the plain
without a raptor's eye, or target set;

a zillion particles of reflected light
upon a journey without destination
with no measured step.

Last Fall

No golds can hold these golds
to the wind's light water,

or burnished coppers, or buffed brass
contain such spun magentas spilling
with the flame fires of their final beacons.

Sand engulfs the drying vein,
vermilion tips to flecks of liver-stain,
while all those dreamed siennas
burn ferruginous with rust;

and tawny footsteps over ochre wafers
scuff and crush.

Tango Bravo, Linaclate

Scooped by moonrush, the bay clutched wind
and the tent arched its spine
at every breath pause
before each shimmy, turn and spin.

My earth-pressed pelvis
holding ground against a heartbeat,
waited for each next advance,
skip, slide, swirl, dip, rotation

through the reeds in closed embrace
to gusts of saxophone, bandoneon,
bow strings quivering to the strain,
a jealous buck-shot spray of rain.

The wild bewitched repulsed, surrenders;
tightens, slackens; beguiles, disdains.
Reaching, retreating, conjoining opposites
return to where they've never been.

Crowdie and Cream

Winter then had the taint of turnip in the milk,
its time marked out by each new orange row
the steaming cattle chomped down to the roots
in neep-muck, slush and rime, until old Abraham
tractored up the deep rut road to once again begrudge
the ticking limit to the electric fence.

All down those shilpit days the porridge and the tea
had a hallowe'en taste of toasted tumshie.
There was turnip too in the mutton bone broth
set simmering up on the anthracite stove,
that mother topped with milk to cool.

I waited for the grass to green on Kirkland Hill,
the gull cloud plough through the turnip field,
and taste restored to sweet and clean
with the fluster of spring in crowdie and cream.

Flitting

Before the current occupiers moved in, they left
to sit at the ruffled edge of neither somewhere or another

inhabiting an imaginary state, perched astride
borders – always waiting, always watching –

migratory birds, alert for the repeating signs
of angled light and temperature which trigger

shifts across some deep immutable instinct of divide,
inducing them to settle temporarily upon a place

that eased away its usual hardened countenance of ice
to let them in, nervous of exposure on emancipated stone,
wary of predators.

It was a ground of murmured promise,
but it was not the promised ground.

They foraged thorn for truths of fruit
preparing for return.

Happit

Outside, grasses spike the windchill and stars are carbon
crystallised in the jammed wheel of heaven.

Trees have been nipped in the bud,
their fingers chisel at the petrified night.

In a landscape without subtlety
hardness can no longer be defined.

Fear not! Fear not! Nothing can come.
Time's iron key clanking in its mortice lock

cannot echo the canyons of dead space
from which no shade can stir.

Inside, a quivering blaze casts us as Javan puppets
shadowing ramayana on the wall.

Coorie doon! Coorie doon, wrapped in firelight,
the scent of pine smoke's sweetening the room.

Coorie doon! Coorie doon, nestled in the groin-warm,
swaddled by the glowing hearth's cocoon.

Outside the mighty universe has stalled
like an abandoned Christmas merry-go-round.

Wetlands

Cloud wipes the moor like a scullery cloth
that never dries; a mildewed caravan
huddles by a breeze-block byre, disused, and
casting slates into the burn's fermenting froth.
Fences rust on the peat bog; pastures pocked
by marsh grass; ancient run-rigs rut the land,
their ditches full of dim. Like a webbed hand,
a tipped tree reaches roots in rigor, locked.

Grieved spirits of the undeparted drape
the stunted hills, and tempt the midday stones
to glisten should a lustre but escape
the lidded sky, allow the land atone
for troubles done; for I could not mistake
that cottage with its plywood blindfold groan.

Falls

Two apple cores
thrown in spate:

one caught in eddies
hugs the bank
bobs beside rage
constrained to wait;

the other   sucked
            rushed
                                    spun
                struck
    plunged
                    swept,
                                        smashed
                immersed
    and
                        re-immersed
            beneath
the falls.

Both cast by chance – not fate
to brown, decay, disintegrate,
are gripped by impetus to oscillate
in calm or rage
through loud relentless
torrents of dead rain.

The Glory

I saw it, I saw it, I swear.
With my own eyes and yours.

Below the summit,
where the sun struck clean
through cascades of vapour,
a congregation of rainbow lights:

four full spectral circles
centred on my startled shadow
cradled in the figment of a cloud.

All the ethereal elements
were gathered round:
the red fire and the yellow earth;
greening Edens of the living air;
lucidities of opened water;
indigo blue infinities of space.

In the forming of the formless,
the appearance of a vanishing.

I blink for hallowed meaning
through the trick lens of reflection
in a thought's unattainable iris,
that was and is, and isn't, wasn't there.

Under Langtang

At Ghora Tabela a sense of homeland
in Himalayan air.

Was it lichens, moss, or pine sap,
compensated latitude? I couldn't tell.

But the lammergeir at Kyangjin
could have been a golden eagle;
that rock-still tahr, a solitary stag
on Buachaille Etive Mor.

Perhaps, before the advent of dogma,
there was a time my ancestors
offered supplication to the wind with juniper,
spun prayers in water to the spirits of immense upheaval.

The potency of mountain here is pure, immediate;
sheer as the ice that tightened in the handhold of the night
to spill its light upon the full intensity of day.

I surge to shout, but hold inside myself the note
to break a morning's soaring silence into cracked cascades.

Langtang Lirung lamplighting the universe,
adamantine pyramid in cerulean sky;

and I am dust in the curve of its carved mantra,
leaving behind all other places, and ghosts of places,
utterly devoid of burden.

Walking To Seannabhat Bay
(for Neil)

Choose a morning breezy with whinchats, pipits, larks,
and a sky of light elisions of blue
that a lochan reflects like a fair eye;

and remember the day is old at eight
in high June over the open moor,
and in the half-night mountains moved nearer
disguised in their still severities of shadow.

Then walk out to the rhythm of a tune that repeats
and repeats in a spiral of presence,
letting your feet make their own decisions
over the debris, peat turf and heather,
respecting the dignity of sundew and butterwort,
and the will to be taken, as water is taken
by the deep inevitability of the grain.

The horizon offers no indication, no obvious direction,
only more horizon; the air imitates the scope of your song
coming and going like the echo of a thought that recurs
and recurs, as it flits and glides to the eastern sun.

The experience of goodness reflecting outward
is calling you forth, and the truth of a longing
released from confusion, imposing no choices,
emerges through sadness to rest in the natural in-between.

Nothing is followed.

Whatever arises leads you on: a subtlety of scent, an
elegance of form, the curve of a lip
as you trace over contours of seductive land,
and all there is before you now
is ocean, cliff, and shell-crush sand.

Sandwood Bay, Gaelic *Seannabhat* from the Norse meaning *sandy lake*

Lochskipport

The water there was clear and dark and deep,
rising and falling in a bowl of rock.
The pier had rotted but for the trusses
bedded to the bottom, barnacle crusted
up to the tidemark, and to which a speculative
creel or two had been tied by turquoise or orange rope.
Bladderwrack drifted, brown with iodine,
slapping the oil of an otter's arc.

The rubble and grit road, scaled and hacked
through schist and gneiss in slices spread with heather
over sphagnum beds and crusts of peat, had been cast off.

A heron went wafting, a mimic in its mirror;
herring gulls shrieked; a bee bummed a butterwort.
The boat that had not yet arrived had sailed.

Summer Carcase in Assynt

the flies come first
greenbottle, fleshfly
flitting through hair
gobbing their pilules
in nostril and ear

then kites and hoodies
rooks on vellum wings
stab at eye and cheek
ravening the carrion
with articulated beaks

the impure meat
scavenged, devoured
in a swarming hum
of thick sweet air
remorseless sun

no blossom here
nor scent of calendula
no moonflower for an absent mind
nor cleansing fire
nor wood to barter for

nature hollows
returns to element
through fungi, bacteria
leaching, dissolving
resolving to stillness

and hardens home
to the last bleached bone
abandoned to last
weathered and cast
on the limestone karst.

Exploring the North West Corner

Mood here is evoked by sky
subliminally from buried stone.
And as this sky is changed in minutes,
so each mood's emotions surface, pass
as halos, shadows, mists across a slope:

the temper of a loch now
duck egg one way, ink another,
peat-pitch, silver, sapphire in between;
a grey hill with its head in cloud
on a lucent morning of brightest prospect.

The mood is mine, or yours.
A rock face wears no weight of loss;
there are no sullen defiles or
glad waters spilling out from desultory pools;
no landscape thrills with expectation

the way I do again and again,
surrendering to this hegemony of heaven,
catching the moods as they arise
from light play on an inland shore,
searching for one I've never sensed before.

Capelaw

Beyond the final gate, the sheep trail burrows
up through heather over ditch bog to a steep dry gully,
where the carved scrapes scratched from rasped turf
serve to coddle huddled yowes from western gales.

I wind the slope at angles, passing rubbed stones, over
bowed grass bleached by frostbite at the end of autumn,
to the upright rusting stanchions left embedded at the top
contorted by long cannonades of wind.

Bonaly loch is black below while all the city sparkles
to the Forth, and hills on hills in silver outlines stretch away;
a tough land in this moment mellowed.
                                        I mouth out poems
to the morning, scrawling sounds that drift by Allermuir,
Caerketton, past the gravel slopes of Scald Law and the Kips:

carved words I scratched for shelter from those storms.

Holding Dunnet

The camera lies.
It doesn't capture as the eye;
all my colours were unwashed.

Where is the cacophony of crows
that filled those trees,
the subtle sulphur tossed up from the sea,
the disturbance of the cut stones
calmed by lichens, moss?

Ten swans swayed
in the cropped field at my back,
fattened for the long flight.

In my pocket
was an almost perfect shell
cupped with a rush of far off waves
and watered light I'd gathered
from its last vast shore.

The Road to Mellon Udrigle

It's always that bit further than you think;
selective memory eradicates
this and that dull dip or undistinguished hump,
the extra mile of dun, dry grasses.

It entices you with glimpses of
a blue-green sea, a blackbird on a fence post
with a pink worm wriggling in its amber beak,
flares of gorse flower sharp as mustard
on the grey dregs of a wintered hill,
the russet limbs in one last stand of pine.

As the light intensifies, I follow the salt
towards the machair on the one track road
that winds and ducks and swings through boulders
cast by vanished ice, defer at passing places
to the slothful coming back, expect that
it should be around the next bend, or the next.

SKINKLES

Peeks

Let's be clear.

Ah ken o' nae particular wey
tae grasp a clarity ayont a' else.

Betimes yon lodestar's solitary licht
micht calm its flichter in a glass;

or the starkness o' a frost describe
a mountain closer than memory;

or water magnify a glister
when its turbulence subsides.

Such luminosity is rare.

Aftimes I breathe a fug o' cloud and haze
an' stir up stoor frae settled layers
that hings a haar about my days.

Gowdcrest in Holyrood

A squall sleets in wi' the nor' west win',
an' we scurry frae the hill
tae deuk alow elder, birk an' pine
ahint a rush o' gorse an' whin.

Aboot oor heids a gowdcrest skips,
a jimpie peen, frae twig tae twig
through oorie spleiters o' glushie rain,
intent on nocht bit grubs and gnips.

Yon slichtest craitur, wi' ne'er a care
fir the grumlie brattles an' loury gurls
that shak oor muckle hairts tae flutter
an' coor in consternation there!

Pearl Earring

1.

A diving boy off Lombok,
living on rough rice,
locked his lungs through seaquakes
from Rinjani's restless roots
to prise an oyster rudely from its bed
beneath a jilaabah of rainbow fish.

Later, an eon of tamed infraction,
calmed to a globule that rolled
in the pink of his mothering palm,
would afford him a cupful of coconut milk
and three quail's eggs in turmeric
for the Idul Fitri feast.

2.

In the steam of an Agra afternoon
by indolent Yamuna
with marble sweat on the dome of the Taj,
a silver thread extruded from a turquoise flame
by teen apprentices is wound around
through drones of Honda, putterings of Bajaj,
to string through necklaces
of trishaw bells and tills
for trinket wages and Laxmi Singh,
jeweller to the Hatton Garden set,
Bollywood, Hollywood, and all the Gods,
or anyone with credit platinum
to render rupees, pounds, or dowry bags of bills
with no regret.

3.
On tarnished Edinburgh
the sun won't strip
from her modest nightgown of freezing fog;
and a dull December Saturday dawns
in late forenoon, where last night's revellers
have tramped a paste of browned off leaves
with a condensation from simmering hops.

Fresh on the mulch,
an earring cast with a single pearl
marooned by a rampant surge of binge
where passions bruised on spirit fire,
and the crook of an elbow eased away
its treasure tale of abandoned loot;
how easily missed and how deftly caught,
where a glitch of silver marks the spot.

Dan

Bottle-loose and fancy free,
Dan, drunk;
a parched dry eye,
a bloodshot tongue
and a boast of last year's stubble,
stumbles,
stained and booted,
through a ten year reek.
cries, *Bastards!*
to his own deserted street.

In the Hermitage of Braid

They gather in packs,
the walkers with their snappers, whelpers,
woofers, cutesy pies, bandy butt-heads,
droolers with protruding labia.

They yell out the names: Sebastian!
Suzie! Rufus! Chloe! Bruteboy! Bernard!

Their necks are weighed with
assorted lengths of studded leads and chains.

Bernard bounds over
and mud paws my chest,
slavering my trousers,
barking like a boom buster.

'Sorry! Excitable!' she proclaims.

'And so am I, you daft bitch!'
I want to reply,
but don't.

Bruteboy bashes on through thistles
followed by the yelping crew.

I shrug, and smile, walk on doggedly,
imagining a stiff staff cracking down hard
on a crazed-eyed skull,
and pause for relief beneath the beeches.

Not a dog walker.
More of a walked dog
marking my way,
pulled down paths I had no urge to sniff.

Edinburgh Façadism

To the front
an open prospect:
fanlight arches,
fine dressed ashlar
Roman columns,
Grecian pediments.

Roon' the back
it's a' closed in:
scabbie windaes,
rough cut rubble,
shite pipes,
same as ony tenement.

A Plague a' Baith Yer Hooses!
A Flyte of Fancy

Wha becomes a Lord or Dame
but fowk wi' dubious claims tae fame
that splash thir cash on various causes –
and write it doon for tax as losses?

Celebrities wi' big personas
wha stick thir self-inflation on us
will get the wink and win the gong –
wi' the richt 'donation' – for a song.

We're tellt it's set by for *those respected
in various spheres* – though unelected,
wha mak thir egos thir careers –
tae populate the house o' peers.

Thir function is tae *strike a balance*
wi' the antics o' a hoose o' chancers
– peddlers o' the party lines
wi' double talk tongues an' gristly spines –

that splatter us wi' spilled opinions
sprayed oot by thir faceless minions
spinnin' wabs o' slick deceit
tae win oor votes and dodge defeat,

whiles grippin' tae thir perks o' poo'er
and influence as they hunker on oor
shunted lives. The democratic choice we've got
is tae suck in air when the beast's at wir throat.

Ye micht as weel be a Lord or Lady
as an upstart athlete or actor, maybe,
wi' the puff tae play it loud an' stubborn.
Whit mair noo dae ye need tae govern?

But thir guile an' gab would ne'er but find
that sacred place o' hairt and mind
if we, the voice that sang the chorus,
renounced thir presumed authority o'er us,

and stood up tae thir feckless rammie
tae wall them in wi' a double whammy
o' human dignity an' truth unwavering,
an' awa wi' thir smug conceit an' havering!

Social Climbing in Edinburgh

Scrambling over the Salisbury Crags,
above Holyrood Palace's royal flags
and the Scottish Parliament, now in session,
presiding over gloom and depression,

I look on up through a daunting cleft
and summon all of my energy left
for a final push on scree and rock
to savour the view at the very top.

I'm told, by nature's divination,
you can gauge the state of grace of a nation.
Auld Scotland's in for a ticklish treat;
there are flying ants up Arthur's Seat!

Diversions

Across the city diversions everywhere:
gas mains here; tram lines there.

Behind their wheels, commuters fiddle
through forty stations of discontent,
and fix themselves in flipped down mirrors
pampering pallors of clamped down rage,
their destinations cut adrift
from tightly tethered spans of time.

Aberration feeds frustration
with the obvious unforeseen;
encountering the extraordinary
reveals more of the same.

A grey road is a grey road, after all,
in mist or rain,
and despite unplanned diversions
destinations never change.

Diversions Revisited

If we could let those chance diversions take us,
as when smoke drifts on an open sky,
instead of fixing our eyes
to the known kerb, strapped in leathers,
we'd see them for what they really are:

other ways that could be our ways but aren't,
in a landscape that would open us,
as a landscape is open to drifting smoke
and the vigorous uncertainty of evolving weathers.

Edinburgh August

It's festival time, balmy and warm,
but winter's coming.

Clark's Shoes is displaying sensible leathers
in preparation for threatening weathers,
when roads fill up with fallen leaves,
and life treads slow and fogs as it b r e a t h e s
through indrawing nights, guarding its feet
from the rigours of venturing out on the street.

Mobile Phone Call on a 33 Bus

Hello! Hello!

Oh cum oan!
Answer the fuckin' phone will ye?....

Hello! Zat you Linda?
Tz me, Denise, aye!
Ah'm on the bus the noo.

Look wull ye dae me a favour?

Ah jist fun oot that there's
A warrant oot this mornin' for ma arrest!

Ah was supposed tae be in court this mornin'
But ah slept in, didn't ah?

Look jist listen tae me, wull ye?
Ah huvnae time tae fuck aboot!

Look ah'm sorry if ah sound short wi ye!
It's jist that ah'm anxious
an' ye ken ma mental condition.

Ah need ye tae get Doctor Newman's number
an' leave a message tae ask him tae send a fax
tae the court tae explain that ah have a mental illness.
an' the reason ah wisnae there wis because
thae pills he gae'd me made me sleep in....

Look ah'm being straight up here....
Thon big clock next tae the bed,
ah had it set right next tae ma lug
an' ah jist slept richt through it.
Ah didnae hear a thing, honest!

An ah'll need the number o' the lawyer.
Oh aye, an' the court tae.
Jist wait a minute!
Hing on, Linda!

HIS ENYBODY GOAT A PEN ON THIS BUS?
LOOK AH'LL GAE YEZ IT BACK, PROMISE!
TA, MISSIS, YER A PAL!

OK, Linda, ur ye still there?

OK, gae me the numbers,
ah'll write them oan the back o' this prescription bag!

Right, aye, ah've goat them!

Naw, ah'm no phonin' them frae ma mobile.
Dae ye think ah'm stupit or somethin'?
They'll trace it, and then they'll ken whaur ah am!

Naw, ah'm no gaun hame!
That'll be the first place they'll look
an' ah'll be sleepin' in the cells the nicht!

Ah'm oan ma way tae a frien's hoose.
Ah'll phone ye frae there.

Aye, it's number 103 South Park Street.
Second floor, second flat. OK?

Look, ah ken it's Friday and it's wan o'cloak!
Phone me back and let me know
if ye goat the message through tae the doctors.

Aye, he likes me an that, so he should dae it.
If no, ah'll phone him frae ma frien's hoose.

OK, Linda, thanks!
Hey, yer a pal, so ye are!

HEY, MISSIS, THERE'S YER PEN BACK!

HO, DRIVER, STOAP AT THE NEXT STOAP, WULL YE?

Picasso
at
The Scottish National Gallery of Modern Art

Excuse me, madam.
In accordance with the policy
of the National Gallery,
could I ask you to please
remove your arse
and place it at your side.

Merchin' Tae Order

Ye want tae've seen the burly beef
gaen roon the toon the day:
prime cuts, hefted, squerrly groomed,
thir sashes crawin' *Best in Show;*

ticht as drums and bricht as whustles,
pedigree stock wi muckle drovers
paradin' doon the High Street for
the red hand o' the abattoir!

Warnings o' Disaster

We've heard stark warnings o' disaster doon the years
frae them that brocht disaster on us:
devout men, greedy, mindless, smug, sincere,
that kent their truths but scugged
thir motives up their sleeves.

This way tae disaster leads!

could jist as weel mean:

Tak it! Or ye micht live tae regret it!

A Richt Conundrum

Ah wisnae fur that
naw.

Ah tellt 'im like
but he was like
well.

An' ah thocht
naw
ye're no' on so ye're no'.

Ah mean
ah wisnae fur it so ah wisnae
no' on yer life.

Bit then again
whit dae ye dae like
when ye're oot o' it
and they're a' at it?

Anent the Kirk's Intent Anent Anent

Tak tent! Tak tent!
The kirk's hell-bent on proscribin' anent.

Lang syne it's scrieved in holy writs
tae document hoo 'oors were spent
in convocation.

Bit noo it's no' got God's consent,
and so they're like tae scrieve:
'concerning' –

which isnae hauf an apt intent
fur nae'ne o' them kent
whit 'anent' meant!

In May 2013 The General Assembly of the Church of Scotland was told that the word 'anent' would be removed from all church documents to make them more accessible.

Shelf Life

Made in Scotland
from finest ingredients.
Best before end:
See bottom

Mobile Phone Call on a 27 Bus

Hi
It's me.
How're ye doing?
Oh fine!

Aye, she's fine too!
I saw her on Friday night.
She was really stroppy, so she was!

Well we were goin' tae the pictures
an' ah told her to turn right instead o' left.
Aye, it's jist her.
She's jist like that!

No, it was the new Bond one!
Quantum of Solace.

No it wisnae ma cup o' tea.
All action macho type stuff.
No' enough seduction for me!

Bit he's my kind o' Bond right enough:
good lookin';
disnae say much.

But ye need mair than that!
Ah've yin o' them at hame!

The Laying Down of Lines
or, Damn the Trams 2010

We prised apart the city's skin,
exposed the tangled networks of its nerves
in gas, electric, telephonic, fibre optic;
tumours in the channels of its drains;
the seepages of substance swallowed, spat;
sophistications fragile as the thirsts induced
upon the inadvertent shutting of a tap.

We recognized the colour codes
in primaries and rust;
the rigging of our evolution
told in layers of functional demand:
pipe upon trench, copper on lead,
hand out of foot, eye over eye, brain within brain.

All that obsolescence seemed quite quaint:
vestigial systems circled by their stars,
a superseded universe of dust
and holes for darkness,
holes for sky and men,
holes for levers, junctions, drills,
for overflows of swept conventions
never likely to be seen again.

We retracted the city's crust,
gazed into our vulnerability,
saw the true extent of our decay,
railed against unwonted extravagance,
the cost of cutting,
longed to cover over, walk away.

The Common Wealth Gains 2014
A reflection on the notion of 'legacy'

Wir feelin' good aboot wirsels,
wi fuckin' are!

Wi've goat it programmed in the ether,
goat it written in the stars
(by a' they scrievers in the media,
if no' the punters in the bars).

They've scoured the docks and built marinas,
pools, parks, precincts, dromes, arenas,
and blawed tae a' the world in shock:
These folk (that's us) *are friendly!*

Oh aye,
wir feelin' good aboot wirsels,
we fuckin are!

Wir new beginners!

Wir nae mair tae be cried as
no mean city boozers, hardmen,
unintelligible, unfit, disadvantaged, bigots,
socially deprived, and *sinners.*

Noo wir tae be fuckin' *winners*!

Ay Fuckland

Fuck!

The fuckin' fucker's
fuckin' fucked!

An' fuckin' noo
ah'm fuckin' fucked

fur ah'm fuckin' fucked
if ah fuckin' ken

hoo tae fuckin' fuck
this fuckin' fucker's fuckin' fucker
tae fuck again!

Fuck!

'Ay fuckland lyke ane furious fornicator',
Sir David Lindsay's description of James V.

Yuletide Me Over
A Christmas Recessional

Hark! If it isnae the skitter, it's the spew.
Sumdae's boaked a veggie curry up the close:
tatties, carrots and peas on earth,
guid will tae a' men!

On Being Served by Pericles in Aldi

No time to speak in deep debate
about the politics of thrift,
the art of commerce in austerity,
the rising price of low fat milk.

At the counter, Pericles exudes a smiling charm.
With sonorous voice he bids me welcome
and continued health to come again – a popular policy -
as, with a mighty warrior's arm,
he swipes the card of the common man,
accepts his coin, and knows his worth.

A check-out line in Spartan times,
while yonder stands the Gorgie polis,
not the grand Acropolis.

Edinburgh Summer
a haarku

Haar! Haar! Haar! Haar! Haar!
Haar! Haar! Haar! Haar! Haar! Haar! Haar!
It's no bloody joke!

A Premonition in Retirement

I dreamed that I'd be there tomorrow
standing in the check-out queue
once the lunch time rush was over,
sometime after half-past two.

And there would be a strange occurrence,
an odd commotion passing through,
then it would revert to normal;
something odd was nothing new.

Well, said someone. *Aye*, another.
It's whit ye'd ca' a richt to-do.
Someone wondered what had caused it.
People shrugged, but no one knew.

I know I'll be there tomorrow
waiting for it, right on cue,
once the lunchtime rush is over,
sometime after half-past two.

Symbiosis and Sin

The presbyterian I was born with
would frown at the way
I lick myself with poems,
if I let him.

He continues to watch me,
the guard in my open prison,
stern, but prudently forgiving;
being an angel would be
too much of an extravagance.

He raises an eyebrow
at the self-indulgence of just expecting
things to work themselves out,
despite the fact that his presence
means I may not expect them
to work themselves out in ways I might want.

It lacks the backbone of ethic,
like a vagrant holding his hand out
on life's pavement from the affectation
of a blanket and a warm dog.
It shouldn't be allowed to succeed.

The things I bank on
are not the wholesome deposits
of endeavour he would nod at.
He wouldn't call them serious money,
and pays no interest, other than
the palpable harrumph he wants me to hear

as I commit another serious fraud to paper.

We are what we are, he and I together.
He can no more change his proper parsimony
into an extravagance of talk
than I can a poem into the wealth of nations.

But, just as the prisoner
is defined by the guard,
the guard is defined by the prisoner.

Though I know sometimes he feels
I should be committed to solitary confinement
when I tend his potatoes
in the gardens of the dispossessed.

A Particular Supplication to The Royal Society for the Relief of Indigent Gentlewomen, Edinburgh

So how do I prove to you
that I really am a Gentlewoman
now that I am indigent,

eh?

The Last Windfarm

Is it nationalist pride,
or the wild goose call?

With one last collective
great out-breath,
soon we'll have lift off
and final clearance.

Through whumping isobars
of Gulf Stream air,
Scotland will fly
towards the Atlantic

in a bold demonstration
of new found power.

Archaepoetry

Thinking leaves no traces
save art and artefact;

a lifetime of crafting,
and could he ever write
just an ordinary stone?

Window Shopper on Princes Street

I had a look around. There were a few things,
but there was nothing really jumping out.
I mean they were *OK*, but I know they were
just not me. It was worth checking, though,
you never know what you'll find. It could
just be exactly what you're looking for,
and if you never looked, well then you would
maybe miss the very thing you're after.

That's what makes it interesting, when you're
just, like, not looking for anything in
particular and you're not really sure,
but you'd know it if you saw it staring
out at you saying, *take me, I'm the one*!
That's what it's all about. Yes, that's the fun.

Park Food Good To Go!

Ice Cream
Slush, Candy Floss,
Donuts, Cakes, Fish 'n' Chips,
Burgers, Hot Dogs, Pizza Slices,
Filled Rolls.

Mobile Phone Call on a Part Route Edinburgh Bus

Elsie? Aye, it's me. No, ah've been away.
Ah jist got back frae Death the ither day.
The weather? Oh, radical, aye, well certainly no'
this grey monotony - though
we did have the odd very violent storm:
the fire and brimstone o' Sunday sermons!
But most of the time it was sunny and warm,
and clear, oh aye, ye could see for millenniums!

Naw, ah went just masel'. Well, they don't do groups,
and it saves ye havin' tae follow the troops.
There's no' many visitors there the noo.
Ah was the only yin, actually. Funny how
when ye're away, though ye wudnae hae thought,
ye look oot for fowk who're in the same boat.
But there was nane in mine that ah came across!

Aye, well maybe, ye know, it was jist because
they were long term residents, domiciles.
And there was me, jist there for a while!
Or else they were travellin' only yin way,
How ah got a return, well ah couldnae say.
Luck, ah suppose. But it was worth every minute.
Such an interesting place! Ye'll never guess whit's in it!

No, there wasnae a pub!
But a'body there was in the best o' spirits.
Ye couldnae get even a bottle o' wine,
but ye didnae need it, 'cos ye felt jist fine.
Ah was laughin' and singin' like a will-o'-the-wisp,

up there dancin' the rumba and twist.
Oh, ye shoulda seen me! Ye wouldnae believe!
Jivin' like a young thing wi' bendy knees!
Oh aye! An' some were flashin' imaginary thigh!
Laugh! How we laughed and laughed, oh my!

Well after the dancin' we'd sit and talk.
There wis nae nicht there; it was licht roon the clock.
And nae clocks either! Ye'd nae sense o' time!
And a very good riddance tae that bloody bind
o' no' bein' able tae freely choose,
and always mindin' yer p's and q's,
like punctuality and queueing for tea!
God, ye've nae idea whit it's like to be free!

Funny ye say that! Ah thought tae pit doon a wee deposit
on a sittin', kitchen, twa beds and a closet.
Nothin' fancy, but handy, and near nice haunts,
where ye'd get oot and enjoy occasional jaunts.
Somewhere tae wipe yer feet on the mat –
Ah wouldnae be needin' mair than that.
A good wee investment, and guaranteed,
for there's only gonnae be an increased need!
Ye've got nae option but tae come the same way,
and once ye're there, well, ye're there tae stay! -
Unless ye wind up jist like me
bein' skooshed back here withoot a by yer leave!
Bit ah searched in vain for first-time-buys.
They looked at me like ah wisnae' wise!
When ye've passed ower there, ye can go whaur ye please!
No this, no that, no those, no these.
It was bloody heaven, perfect peace!
And certainly beats a week in Dumfries!

Well ah'm no' quite sure jist how ah got hame.
It went sae quickly. Remember that pain afore ah departed?
When ah got back it was like it'd never started!
Ah hae mind o' them puttin' in that drip,
and then ah was off on a lovely trip.
Nae need tae think about needles in veins,
or chemicals jist like they pit doon drains!
And yer hair fallin' oot in handfuls and wads
and wonderin' if ye would beat the odds.
Nae pingin' machines, nae pulses and pressure!
Nae ice packs! There ah wis, like a lady o' leisure!
When you're wantin' misery, ye ken where tae find it.
But happiness, well, it's like bein' blinded -
in a nice sort o' way. Ye don't *have* tae look.
Visions come tae ye like scenes in a book.
When ye're back frae Mallorca, well ye're no' quite here
for a day or two. Bit *this* is different. It'll no disappear!
It stays right wi' ye a' the time.
Ah've never felt jist sae perfectly fine.

Oh, aye, on the way back ah thought ah was dreamin'!
There was this traffic warden schemin'
and handin' oot fines on motorbikes.
Imagine! You've never seen the likes!
For nane of thae riders wis comin' back:
they'd a' gone forever doon the track.
In Death they'll find that especially funny,
for the cooncil 'll no be gettin' their money!

Right, cheerio, then!
When we meet it'll be like ye hardly knew me.
That is if ye dinnae jist look right through me!

From Fundament to Firmament

You recognise it when the signs change
from block bold to cursive; necessity to delicacy;
essential to complementary, alternative, artisan,
designer, bespoke; to profit, from loss.

To profit from loss, flit from grub to cuisine
as life-styling butterfly, naturally selected,
selecting the natural through self-cleaning glass:
one wildflower garden, delivered on time.

We've moved from the coal scuttled open hearth fire
to eco-sustainable wood burning stove.
Enclosed in our crucibles, sirens rush past beyond hedges
and fences, screaming alerts as they fade to the south.
Down in the reed beds the same shit flows
from fundament to firmament, the way of desire.

Which Art In Heaven

Art
Art is
Art is anal
Art is an ally

Give us this day our artisanally baked bread...
and forgive us our debts.

Glasgow Droppings

I took a stroll around George Square
to see whose heads the pigeons shat on:
Peel, Scott, Watt and Robert Burns,
Victoria, Albert, various commons.

The shit seemed heaviest on Gladstone's head,
as if those birds knew just the weight to press
upon those cold cast shoulders,
the hair turned white with filtered pickings
cast out from the people's pokes
and scattered with the easy grace
of hands bestowing inedible bread.

Hard Cheese!

My mother swiped flies
saying *Get to France!*
I now realise this was Glasgow polite
for *Get tae f...uck!*

My mother was wise,
it's better with *France*:
the flies there make love without any respite,
on Abbaye de Bellocq.

Just Daydreaming

Walking down Dalry Road
this lady on the pavement
went weaving in front of me

left
        then right
then left
        then right.

I couldn't get
            past

despite a flurry of shuffling steps.

She stopped and turned,

I'm sorry, son!
Staggering there
all over the place!

This being Edinburgh,
she added, though,

But I am not drunk!

Jist
        daydreamin'!

Fresh Snow

It confronts me with buried truths
I'd bury again to place a foot
where I know no foot should go:
imprints of ego on status quo.

Life won't halt.
It piles up with the burdens I impose on it,
impossible as wet cement,
passing through gestures of grit and salt.

We take to bed for warmth;
and still it's falling,
without guilt for purpose,
from a sky that holds no opinion.

Always That Colder Cold

Winter
of sixty-three.
I could skite on my erse
doon Glebe Hill wi nae rips in my
breek cheeks.

French Kiss, Marchmont

She was French, I remember,
but, like a star in some black and white movie,
I can't call back her name.

Only her eyes, her hair,
and the coming together of tongues.

I was so infatuated
I must have blown it round
the streets and steely skies
of that December's drawn in days,
the blackened cut outs imitating trees,
the frothy slush that should be snow
across the city's public ways.

We made love in a box-room for the heat,
shivered at the speed with which
coffee turned cold and formed a milky sludge
upon the surface of a half drunk cup.

Talking Native

Dropping off Caerketton Hill
for minutes we approach each other
and I want to say:

My god,
what a wind up there raging on the ridge,
and warm from the south!

It scooped me like a hammock,
took crows like feathers,
pulled apart heather,
forced open pores!

But, wrapped up tight,
the culture's saying,

Naw, naw.
That's no it at aw.

and as we draw nigh
I keek at the sky and say:

Aye, aye.
It's no half a braw blaw the day.

Ootby

Ah hae min' o' a fella there yince
wha couldnae dae't.

An' he wis richt sair
and scunnert, so he wis,
fur he couldnae thole the thocht
o' them a' bletherin' he wis a footer
an' cryin' him no wyce.

An' a' the time it wis jist that
he hadna got the hang o't
an' he didna ken it wis
a' doon tae him no hanlin' it richt
so it widnae jist gang
the wey it wis supposed.

Yince he fun' oot, min' ye,
ye couldnae ha'd 'im back.

There's a wheen o' weans
aboot the toon
ye wudnae keek at twice
tae ken thir faither.

Angus Tea Room

The ladies wear their bracelets, and their hair
done neat enough to gossip over tea
and scones; their menfolk sit across the way,
shaved close, they stare at middle distances,
their hard hands grip their cups, their weathered cheeks
with bloodlines stiffen now and then, release
a word to ease the tension of their air
against the dishes and the cutlery.

Dressed for the coffee shop in blouse and skirt,
or straight pressed trousers and well ironed shirts
and ties with pullovers and polished shoes;
the ladies laughing, and the men bemused
now that retirement has arrived at last
and occupies this present with that past.

The Sound of Iona
August 6 2014 Noon

hush hush
slip sloch
tweet tweet   caw caw
peewit   whoo whoo
                             moo moo
    croo croo   baa baa
    swish swash
    ska ska
    skeet skeet skeet   crunch crunch
                                                              bow wow
  drip drop   woof woof
  drop drip   munch munch
  drip drop
    drip
                    buuuzzzzzzzzzz

phut phut   rumble rumble   clank clunk   ding dong

Ladies and gentlemen,
all passengers may now disembark by the central ramp.
On behalf of Caledonian MacBrayne,
we'd like to thank you for sailing with us today.

shuffle shuffle   click click   peep peep   tinkle tinkle

mea mea
agnus dei
gloria in excelsis deo

jingle jingle!

The Shock of the Mocked

Iona Abbey's seven poun' entry
keeps oot the riff raff and lets in the Gentry.

The riff raff built it wi' sweat and skill,
but noo tae get in they must rattle the till.

And if that's no' enough tae gie them pains,
it's four poun' thirty for each o' their weans!

The riff raff built it for God in his glory,
but noo it's (p)reserved for Scotland's Story,

and the elevation of whit's lang past,
no' the revelation of whit will last.

I am the way the truth and the life,
through me is the answer tae a' yer strife!

So they were telt, and so they believed,
but the truth is it meant hae'n their pockets relieved

tae enter the sanctuary of the livin' God,
fur they'll no' get in if they're no' weel shod,

as they'll need tae be for the life's been shed,
and they'll walk on in doon the Way o' the Dead.

Passing Craighouse

Those who survive will overgrow like this,
returned to wildness,
sequestered in plywood,
eyebrows gone astray.

Only the bats that occupy their eaves
will call reprieve on demolition.

The tidy world that would preserve abhors decay,
but, sapped of effort, serves its notice and is apt to say
the dereliction's nature's gentle rot at play,

leaves the developer to have his way.

Wiping Out Graffiti

It's a lost cause
like honest banks.

When you write on the walls,
write poetry.
Thanks!

Scaffolding

One December dawn the rigger gang came
echo-sounding the town with bangs and clangs
of alloy pipes and planking, slang harangues,
slung hammers, spanners, clunking chains,
anchor-drills shrilling through stone clad walls.
The gaffer, clamping his weight to a brace,
swung up on one arm with all of the grace
of an acrobat bowing to cat calls.

They framed the tenement to stand on crutches.
A functional prosthesis now attracts
attention to its frailty – touches
of its ailing we ignored, despite the cracks.
Now they've locked it in a covered cast,
to segregate its present from its past.

At the Parliament for Independence

On the pavement outside
a four hundred million year old fossil bides its time;
a fish that swam Silurian seas
caught in such wee momentous times as these!

Installation
from an installation in the Water of Leith by Antony Gormley

The iron man stands in the river
under the hanging tree;
lapping around his hollow ankles
sounds in his empty head;

cast to nakedness, bronzed by rain,
his rust-stained eyes are resting spots
for dragon flies.

He's gazing past the hidden face,
the one that masks the pain,
gazing at another place
of no defined horizon.

I watch him,
blinking, from the dripping wood,
those dimpled waters moving on,
the drainpipe fingers curving down,
his manhood rigid, limp;

an effigy laid bare to passing rubbish,
dropped debris, the rising flood,

designed to be toppled by torrents.

The Summation of Desperate Dan

I am always
centring things
adjusting the slanted
realigning the slewed
smoothing the ruffled, the lumpy, the rumpled
arranging the sloughed off
stiffening the slouched
amending the erroneous
rectifying the awry
gathering up the fallen
rounding up the stray
scrubbing the grubby
restoring the stained
touching up the scuffed up
tucking in the hanging out
chucking out the clutter
tuning in the out of kilter

meticulous to a fault
I organise the exact locations of all my useful things
preserving them against a day that won't rain hard enough
upon that splattered glass I can't look through without
the nag that lifts me onto ladders with a sponge

I order my thoughts on well swept stairways
I wash all my utensils after use

but *command* me to conform

and   I'll be u n
                con   vention al
        con
trary
                re   bell   ious
    swim   s
            i
            d
            eways against the t
                              i
                              d
                              e   at an unGODly hour

                    o
            c   a   s in the   cos
                h   mos

            matching

                                    your

                        FORCE

                                    with

                my

                        POWer

A Protestant Reflection On Redundancy

Laziness exhausts me:

a' that struggling wi' guilt and shame,
self-admonition for a waste o' time an' space
only makes me want tae sleep;

a' that rising up
in opposition tae the righteous world o' busyness,
biting at its feeding hands,
inventing a' the arguments o' blunt contrariness,
jist fags me oot;

a' that rummaging for comforts, pampering,
deciding whit an' how tae eat an' drink,
or read, or play, or lie an' gawk at
is a perfect pain in the neck;

a' that futile effort it requires
tae switch it aff, ignore it, numb it doon,
or bury it beneath a pillow wi' yer head
comes back tae suffocate ye when ye wake.

Ah'll pander nae mair tae its outrageous demands!

From here on in, ah vow tae channel a' that energy
towards bein' too determinedly indolent
tae be bothered by laziness at a'.

But, God, it takes it oot o' ye daein' nowt.

Takin' the Piss *(In Full Flyte)*

On the decision to reduce funding for public conveniences in Edinburgh in order to make 'vital budget savings'. The Scottish tradition of 'flyting' is the exchange of insults conducted in verse.

Edinburgh,
I hae walked a' yer ways
doon streets and trails, oer hills and braes,
stravaiged alang yer wynds and closes,
wi' gaits geology imposes.

But haud!
Afore I'm whisked awa'
wi' whit's ahint yer venerable wa's -
reserve, tradition, erudition, airt,
the enlightenment o' lads o' pairts -

ken this,
despite nae mean achievements -
yin loyal dug, and snatched bereavements -
history teaches ye were aye remiss
wi' conveniences for yer burghers tae piss.

Indeed,
I'm tempted wi' the theory
ye built each vennel dark and drearie
tae stymie fowk in licht frae seein'
ilk body staunin' in there peein'!

Times past
ye had a reputation
as the reekie capital o' the nation,
an' no jist for the smoke frae flues,
but ordure heaps and midden stews.

But noo,
when sleek electric trams
whoosh by alang yer tree-lined strands
an' polis boxes serve coffee an' tea,
it's a sair fecht tae find a WC!

It seems
as if yer new fund fame
for cultural splendour - no' lack o' drains! -
has coaxed ye tae be laith tae spoil it
by the rank intrusion o' a toilet

and a'
the bother that entails
wi' infrastructure and access rails,
facilities tae chainge a baby,
hygiene, cleaning, health and safety!

That's a'
very weel for City Chambers,
where marble urinals avert the dangers
ye're in when oot on an evenin' walk
an' wind up tyin' a knot in yer cock;

or worse,
if ye happen tae be a lady
cross-legged and hobblin' unco unsteady
tae duck doon tae the Water o' Leith
in search o' a bush tae find relief.

Wi' smeddum
we stride through the Caley hotel,
whiles actin' like we're well-heeled swells,

fur a body's forced tae be richt savvy
an' ken a' the tricks tae find a lavvy.

The worst
o' it is yer city thrives
in pourin' liquid at wir lives!
God forbid that we micht think
there's nae whaur tae piss, sae we'll no hae a drink!

Lord, naw!
Lost sales o' whisky an' beer
wid cost yer coffers o'er dear,
and yer civic expenditure wouldnae gae far
withoot hogmanay parties an' festival bars.

Noo mair
an' mair we're forced tae rely
on the vagaries o' the Lothian sky,
an' bidin' oor time until it rains
and washes awa' the urine stains.

Enough!
Ye're makin' yer pensioners triggers
tae boost yer use o' amenities figures,
but ye ken why they're there as soon as ye see them
raxin' through libraries, galleries, museums!

Yin o' them
tellt me a frien' o' a frien'
went doon tae the cooncil tae mak a scene,
for she'd heard if she went there tae whine and nag
she'd get fitted wi' a free colostomy bag.

There's trees
an 'poo bins' for ilk Embro dog,
but whaur dis the dog walker fin a bog?
May Him that pairted the waters judge ye
for the lack o' a basic public cludgie!

In this age
o' the internet much has chainged,
but, fegs, ye canna yet pee online!
There's apps tae tell ye the time o' each bus,
Whaur's the maps o' the stairwells tae squat when needs
must?

Rouse up now
and tax yer flush banking sector
for a slush fund tae sweeten yer tight-ersed electors!
In the name o' nature, grant them thir wish,
and gie them the places tae shit an' pish!

My Scotia

Auld stane wall.
Scrievit on the lintel:
FEAR GOD ONLYE

Liberty and thrall.
Says it all.

The Blackie at the Dawn o' Day

I bide for you in the still-dim o' an efter-rain
that allows the blinter o' ane misslie star,
or icy planet, tae glory through afore the dawn,
whiles tholin' the cauld o' a nicht's glaur dyin'.

For I'm a' the warmth that's snauchled here noo,
ettlin' for your ither, sma'er warmth tae sing
frae a thicket, the stark sticks o' yon barren gean,
thae first upliftit notes o' spring.

Mobile Man on a 19 Bus

Yes
Aha
Yes
Yes?
Oh, yes!
Yes aha aha
Yes
Yes
Yes
Aaaah
Mmmmh
Oh
O.K.
Yes
Aye
Aha
Aha
Yes
Yes
Yes
O.K.
Yes
Aye
Bye!

Hi pal.
Aye, she called.
Ah just said naw.
Cheers.